Colours
in Chiaroscuro
and other poems

**Colours in Chiaroscuro
and other Poems**

© Copyright: Keith Harris

Published by *Pending Press* Ltd. in 2010

Cover picture © Dafydd Davis-Hughes

ISBN 978-1-903466-03-2

Printed and bound in Great Britain by www.direct-pod.com

Contents

Preface

Once I wrote a novel and sent it to an literary agent. He wrote back saying, "This is in some ways a 'unique' book," but then he added, "Yet so many people nowadays write about their upbringings."

Mm, it was a novel. The narrative had very little connection with my own life.

Though I would prefer not to write a preface, I have decided not to risk the reader assuming the 'experiences' described here are my own in a superficial or outward sense.

In contrasting his own work with a contemporary practitioner of their art, John Keats wrote, "He writes about what he sees, I write about what I imagine".

Need it be added that Dante did not have to visit the Inferno in order to write about it. Neither did Shakespeare have to go to Verona to embrace Juliet's love or Scotland to live inside Macbeth's experience of time shorn of the meaning of the present – *Tomorrow and tomorrow and tomorrow* ...

A lot of poetry written today is set within the scenery of objective circumstances – and there is nothing to criticise in this. But another tradition of poetry also exists whose stage is that of the imagined experience.

Dedication

This book is dedicated to
the One it was always dedicated to

Miscellaneous Poems

May a star shine on our meeting ...

Who am I

Who am I
in the hours' habitual demise,
who am I
in slighting phrase where words
sound loudly
over mutely musing mood,
who am I
in tear-filled laughter lorn with
comedy's subtle bereavement,
who am I
in Winter's star-stabbed sable
far, far infinity
camouflaged in frosty breath
distance unattainable
dark and old,
who am I today
tomorrow who am I?
Who am I
in time's untethered trickling
and in this sheer and gentle
quest where
question and the one
who quests
are one,
who am I – my
questioning flames
behind the sturdiness of now
to bear even my footfall,
softly as a cherry blossom's
spiralling descent,
down onto the stony, piercing
certainty
of hallowed ground
... who am I?

My Daughter

Proudly biting her plastic toy,
she hasn't learnt to talk
and hasn't learnt to walk
but her eyes looking into mine
tell me why –
why I went into the café that day
and there, by chance
as they say,
first met the girl who became
her mother.

Two Short Poems

Chomping luscious green
a caterpillar
creeps toward
the chrysalis

* * *

unmotivated
by the chrysalis
the burnt moth
crawls

Iron Wheels

Only fingertips
parted by plate-glass
kiss farewell –
iron wheels outpace her feet
iron wheels, iron wheels …
a hand sighs in the wind
carriages blur into landscape
tears coalesce with autumn rain.

The Appointment

Their breathing visible in frost-cold air
pall-bearers dressed
in black and bloated overcoats.
A coffin lowered jerk by jerk.

Behind black lace, tight grey hair
and tighter features
trembling
his widow wonders, "Why,
why all that hassle, shouting, slamming doors,
no goodbye kiss –
so much haste to make the plane
that crashed".

His few friends among acquaintances
gather shivering
to see a shovelful of frozen earth
tossed
a man´s height down below
the icy ground onto
a finely varnished wooden box.

A Fool's Hope

Hope cocooned in hardship –
in black space a glint of
starlight untainted
by sundry concerns
and Mordor's breeding desolation.

Hope's absence outweighs
her perennial nativity
even as the background of spacial nothingness
outmeasures starlit points shimmering
in night's unblemished beyond ...
far, far above sorrows of Middle Earth

Sam and Frodo's numbers –
non-significant decimals
in the statistical diagnoses
of the tower of power.

A Blind Leper's Wish

I wish or write
because I can no longer wish
nor speak as in my mouth pus
oozes from swollen sores.
Words are mumbles
(are they mine?)
Stumps in blotchy scar
fingers (were they mine?)
writing only with
and within muteness.

I wish a leper's wish whose flesh
rots on his cheek
whose odour makes putrid
all other scents,
who lives among joys of men
but does not live their joy.

I wish, I wish a blind man's wish
who yearns ever for
the face of man
but does not see her face.

I want to live, I want to love
in fair love´s inmost hour.
I wish a blind leper´s wish
where from this sightless
lonely cloistering
jumbled noises blare and fade
in meaningless to and fro,
where fervent murmurs frolic
far beyond a leprous reach
and voices beckon
only to retreat,
where the living touch
is met by scab
… and nearness is
only a silent unborn child.

But What If ...

Ah, the sunset I'll go out and look –
just a minute the tea
the wife and the kids and the TV ...
Oh, it's dark
dark, dear me,
was it
was it the sunset
was it the sunset I was going to see?
Ah well, tomorrow
tomorrow there'll be time –
or will there be?
Will it be rainy, cloudy
impossible to see –
next week
next week then –
but what if, but what if ...

Flames

Two candles approaching
thresholds of their fire
with staccato suddenness
flame as one –
drawing apart they separate
as abruptly,
each flame shines
now for and from itself
even as their fires when together
burn in beautiful union.

* * *

Lost

Is hope born from dying?
For with each encounter I die
and become (a lesser
or a greater?) joy-filled
or sorrowing self.

Norms glare poisoning
my heart's impatient purpose
as my little earthen ego
wanders through its own uncertain
never-starting story.

Is your human presence
embroidering my consciousness
and unconsciousness hundreds
or thousands of inexplicable instances
each day and sleepless night ...
is this you in me
but insignificant subjectivity?

Bordered by waves of curling hair
your face and uniquely coloured eyes
gateways to an I
alive in outer day ...
yet those same eyes alive
in my inner sight
gaze back at me
to leave my heart blushing
with new-discovered innocence.
Is the I in you
alive in me?

Two lives you live:
one known by day
and one unknown in me.

Are you out there
and me imprisoned, bound
by this blunted body, divided
by a no-man's tract of norm
from your daytime you?

If the you-in-me
is not you
then who am I?
(And who are you?)

This she, I speak of you
in the more objectified
dispassionate and grammatically
incorrect third-person singular,
this she – held in my heart
as the fairytale princess beyond
the grasp of grown-up rationality
games of give and take
and dour daytime circumstance –
is she
is she fantasy?
(And am I the fool
who never spoke his lines?)

Whether you smile and say, "Hello"
or glance away,
whether I see you everyday
or do not see you
for a year and a day
and a bit more –
still I see
the you who no one sees
but me, still in uncountable
instances each everyday
I see you in my
inner vision
looking back at me.

I have whispered to you
called your name in endless
endless hours fore the dawn,
I have spoken your name (with choking
voice and tears noted by none)
in spaces shorn of sense
in spaces separating heaven
from my earthly self –
into that very invisible room
between
you and me.

I want nothing.
I have lost all.
My dreams are in coma
lifeless as anaesthetized limbs
under the laser-sharpened surgical knife.

I have turned away refusing
with proud objectivity to let
you take part in me.
Many times I ran
and ran from you,
many times I ran and ran
from you in me
but always left behind
my self.

Prising you from my heart
leaves a gap in me,
my being self-estranged
and less than whole
for whom 'to cherish'
is a word deleted from
my active vocabulary.
The only healing (it would seem)
for you to be in me
but then my inner and my outer
lives remain unwed.
(Where do I end
and you begin?)

Am I lost to you
as you are lost to me?

Is hope
the hope of sleep
the hope of not to be?
The Sleeping-Beauty sleep
where years and sequential time
move on and on
without me,
where I (who long for you)
am not – is this hope
or the mute destructive
force of hopelessness?

I have no answer.
Will I never find you,
will you never speak
to me nor I
to you?
Will I never know
if you
and you alive in me
are one
or two?

Are my feelings for you
subtle, gentle gifts
heartening your life?
Or are these unsettled yearnings
unwanted and intrusive breaches
of my consciousness in yours,
lassos of entwined longings
whirling round your inner life?
Or is my subjective you
– the you in me –
forever segregated
from you?

Am I doomed to live
the Thomasian dilemma
of the twin without his twin?

I am disheartened
dead even to the reflection
of romance, dead
to myself
and thus to you.
Is my only hope
the Sleeping-Beauty sleep –
dreamless disappearance
of both me
and you in me?

Hopelessness seeping into hope,
hope flickering in hopelessness –
ripples within ripples
harmony and disharmonies sounding
through time and timelessness.

Are you lost in me
as I am lost in you?

Yet when I wake from dying
embers of the day before
in ashes of unanswered separation –
new hope is lively burnished
cascades of joy surface
from a sea of gratitude
for I have seen you!
(I have seen you
in my inner seeing)
And as ever
you look wonderful.

Virtually Tragic

The Eye of Mordor
printed on the dollar bill?
Or the US one more fall guy
doomed to deficit?
Its Moral Majority without a fig-leaf
of Welfare,
its future prisons
mass-produced and manned
only by machines
for inmates from the ghetto
while bankers' derivatives
screw profits out of
phenomenal sub-prime pursuits
money made from loans they
(and everyone else) knew
weren't going to be paid back –
thin-air profits bought and sold
on math-magic markets.
Bankers are barons
in the Münchhausen mould.

Profit poured into poisoned debt
so the banks' balances bounce
rudely out of the black
and our taxes are used to bail-out
what (they say) mustn't be allowed
to fail ... people squeezed
to pay bankers' bonuses –
so fat-cat accounts swell up again
as the latest GMO fast breeder.

Investment bankers went one better
than wartime whores who smudged rouge
on ageing ashen faces to make them ruddy,
the prostitutes turned grey to sickly pink
the bankers made black as red as blood
by buying loans they knew were toxic as dioxins –
in games of musical chairs they hoped
not to have to face the music
standing up and holding
mounds of derived debts.
But when the music stopped they
were all together holding onto one another
(and one another's debts)
the chairs had disappeared
and loans proved as reliable
as the climber's clutch on thin air.
(Only Baron Münchhausen
could pull himself up by his own pigtails!)
Bankers' hands were dripping blood-
red ink to change the
colour of black bank balances.
Who gets to pay, well
just guess, it's just you and me
and every man on the street
earning dollars by the hundreds.
Investment bankers too have bonuses in hundreds
only theirs are hundreds of thousands,
those more responsible get millions
while those most responsible of all
at the very apex get bailed out with billions.
Unless of course its just digits – digits
deriving digits, numbers churning numbers
where the wealthy, win or lose,
always stay well-off
only working women lose their work and wonder
if there's Welfare.

The Twentieth Century's raw and war-torn
tragedy and hope
transposed to a global rondo:
tragedy, hope and
virtual tragedy
derived from the glutinous derivation
of derivatives.
How about registering your disapproval
by buying rouge for hoary
(or is it whore-y)
investment bankers' faces?

The Knight*

As his horse's hooves
clip-clop cobble stones
a lithe and barefoot maid with
longing look seeks
the eye within the helm.

* This little poem, originally without a title, was taken from *Armoured to Anonymity*.

A Sensitive Chaos*

Tremors
from a soundless bow
string reverberations
through a system's faltering
periodicity ...
in banal tempestuousness
a babe beckons
the womb.

* This poem was originally taken from *Cupid's Anon*.

Avalon*

When song to imagination is intoned
in Avalon the ancient way is honed –
awake in starry Summer climes
maid and man without their shoes
seek sacrament in sweet débuts:
behind those sleepy bedtime chimes
when now, to a happily-ever-after cue,
our prince and princess sigh to woo.

* This poem was originally taken from *Colours in Chiaroscuro*.

Two Metaphysical Poems

Time out of (or inside of) Time

Is it possible to be within time,
to be inside time's inmost becoming?
For me to be within time
must mean to be within –
within what? Not the past
for the past has gone by
so how can I
be within what has already been
and gone? Not the future
for the future has not come
and is therefore nothing
but a not-yet-been, a 'non-event'.
What is left?
Only now.
But the now is an infinitesimal,
a divide between what's gone
... and what is coming,
a boundary which makes the pico
second seem an aeon,
an aeon to the power of an aeon
to the power of an aeon to ...
A point without inwardness
is this my experience of now –
something gone, already passed even
as it appears? Or
is my present spacious?
Can I live inside a boundary?
Can I live inside the thickness
of a mathematical line?

The point of the present
can be defined by one line
crossing another; two lines
without thickness cross
or spear through each other to
mark the moment of the now.
And since time's inexorable ongoingness
is the arrow of the horizontal line,
the crossing line is vertical.

As my experience of now
is spacious and as the divide
between past and future
is without space, no thicker
than the thickness of a mathematical
line, is not my life
within time, within the now,
an experience of the vertical?

In the vertical line what is
to happen later is already
taking place within my consciousness.
My heart is pierced
by the future,
even now I am alive
a little further into the future
– and the miracle is
there is no collision,
my experience of what is to come
and what comes
is continuous coalescence,
I am living the future in the now.

As the foot treading upon the serpent's head
time's hidden vertical crosses
the slithering of earthly ongoingness.
The future present
in the human experience of now
christens
nature's crowded struggling
for existence.

In this spacious present
the monad is
conscious of life within space
and simultaneously
conscious of itself.

Those who look
longingly toward the heavens
have chosen well:
the symbol of our human earth is
a cross over a circle –
the cross erected upon a skull.

Animal Time

The sparrow dives
to the ground and darts
its glance toward a tree then
straight away toward me, its eye
and head twitch hither, thither
here, there, everywhere
and then quite suddenly
it thrusts up and flies away.
Does, or how does, the sparrow
experience now?
Does it not dive toward
the present moment but
at its touch its consciousness
is vanquished –
only another twitch
another dive to reach
the present
and then another and another –
touching the moment only
to lose itself?
Is not the sparrow's experience:
rapid-fire chaotic points of nervy
disconnected present moments?

What of the cow (or the bull
if unaffected by the urge
to find its female kind)?
Chewing the cud the cow
ruminates and ruminates
within the passage of the day,
she neither lives nor dies in
the present moment because
for her time goes quietly, quietly by.

What of the lion, does she
experience the drama of the moment?
Assuredly, for she hunts –
before the chase all of her
her eyes, whiskers and waiting limbs
look
to the moment of attack
off she rages pounding into
the leap her
claws bring blood, jaws bite – in
the moment of the kill
she lives the drama
(or the presence) of the present.
But after gorging
how does the lion pride
pride itself on life?
His mane magnificent
his body cushioned in warm comfort
he would purr
the very moment of the now
... but only falls asleep.

What animal can return
the human eye, what beast
or bird can return the glance
of human certainty?
Not the bird which nervously twitches
and darts only to die in the moment,
not the cow which chews
and chews and chews,
not the lion which kills, rips and swallows only
to sleep – not the ape, monkey or chimp
for their eyes are elsewhere
they cannot return my eye
(cannot mirror my I)
cannot retain the now in time.

Animal time dissects:
lives and dies in the moment
or chews and ruminates ongoingness
or chases and kills – only to pass
purring into slumber.
The darting discontinuity
of unconnected moments,
the continuous contented continuity,
the hunter which longs to kill
and find its deeper meaning in
falling into sleep.

Only human time knows
unity in the trinity –
where the kiss of past and future
lives within the lancing
of now.

Armoured to Anonymity

Armoured to Anonymity is a sequence of linked poems.
The setting, nominally at least, is Arthurian Celtica.

The poems deal with a rider's attempts to combat darkness in the outer world and in himself by following the lonely 'Arthurian' quest. And perhaps they also deal with the relationship between 'day' and 'night'.

1

Armoured to anonymity a lonely rider
whose path his destiny decides.

2

Through wilderness and towns, through crowds
and restrictions and divisions
of families, races, nations, guilds
... and on to pass unnoticed behind
a solitary homestead in the hills
as the West's rosy shimmering
slips toward the sea
and dark quietens unsteady colour.

3

Iron-clad and mounted
on the grey and foamy mare
leading the trusted sandy steed
upon a gently inclined weaving
ancient way
not overgrown though little used
and bordered by new green
from where white flowers face
the cloudless blue and fragrant
shrubs offer the wayfarer
refreshing sense.

His gaze wavering in distances
back to the tradesmen's bustle
and the towns then on
toward lonely Celtic moors
where mountains and seaborne mists
mean movement in the lonelier life.

4

From afar he trails a diligent trail
from whence day is freed in rosy dawn
to whither eve's magenta bows
toward the midnight sun.
And his ascending once more
... descends
to mourn with each new morn.

By sunlight riding further
alone and on,
threading with his self
through day's display ...

to abide in dusk-awakened scents
beside the moonlight's wavy musing
and the music of a Celtic mere.

5

Memories break as waves
throughout his trials to step
determined steps to where –
to where his knowledge never tells.
But behind his visor
chancing change
behind his breastplate
changing chance.

6

He reins in his charging steed
to graze on greens near homes
of men half-cleansed from grime
as nature's rearing day
dwindles to stillness
quietly, quietly
near dwellings in sleep's familiar ways
where women loosening the grind
labour with the lasting child.

7

His countenance a visor as he rides
to divest his days of that stealth
which lurked around his crib
and clung to his tear-strewn way into
childhood sleep – and which still
masks riddles in his livery unless
the shadow in himself is faced.

8

Unknown he rides through
those years when youth
stalked by an umbra of ugliness
becomes no longer young.

9
Riding lightly to joust
through unplanned day on an
unarmed steed's easily
harnessed way.

10
He gallops his pounding
stallion with pounding
heart to the clash
of lance on steel –
in defeat:
a pauper's clod of earth
and perhaps a poor maid's sigh,
in victory:
a slight dig of spur
flanks out his further flight
toward his further frays ...

11
On a main bridleway through Caledonian forest
sharp sunlight's motifs mottled and moved
by birch-leaf in the breeze – as well-attended
damsels, beggar monks and traders whipping
heavy-laden mules pass by
the steel upon the horse.

In unsteady shades fantasy plays
upon the passing moment and into
troubled sleep as they
dream of life behind
the visor and the shield.

12

Dappling chances dulled in sense
how many days, disjointedly, dreamed by
while wonder glanced
his heart against half-meetings
(brooding with presences)
of people unknown
and half unknown.

13

As mud splashes
from his trotting mount upon
the clogs of surly thickset men
who tightly grasp their bags.

14

As his horse's hooves
clip-clop the cobble stone
a lithe and barefoot maid with
longing look seeks
the I within the helm

15

Saddle proud rides and the norm
of easy victory
let moments march away
into sequential and unsubjected time –
but cannot cause nor erase
his seeing in sight
nor shut that sheltered door
from where a knocking echoes
with the stars of night.

16

Rumours of falsity and privilege
spit from the ignorant mouths
of those who shun to learn.
But when crude foes tailored
to joust and plunder daughter's wares –
or when things crawl
from heathen heaths and fears
creep through hamlets cringing
near the mere's swirling haze –
or as anarchy plunges
all to war against all
... then
led by his steed's prophetic step
Arthur's knight from night
appears upon the ridgeway
a silhouette
who silently heralds
the rising sun.

17

Is he young
or stern and scarred of cheek
none knows – his visor
blocks his visage,
he rides to battle in our Table's name,
only upon his seat in Camelot
does his own ever newly inscribed
name
gleam with gleding gold.

18

Behind his visor chancing change
behind his breastplate
changing chance –
where destiny decides with easy rein
his deed's anonymous amour
there plays to undecide.

19

Each rider, fresh as arterial redness
flowing through craving limbs,
swoons into slumber
as knightly dusk rolls nightly over day.
Is there a smile upon his sleepy face
or grim fatigue – none knows
for darkness drowses overall;
his efforts have fought his day
his night needs grace-filled sleep.

20

Polarity twines his moments
in freehood's fighting fold:
tight recall of knightly oath
in iron rounds of iron rush
as sword and lance clash
with the well-worn shield
– and paths where hope faints
into silences before
his wanderings approach the Castle
(of the Rose in twilight's womb)
whose night's suffer none to pass
except that he be called.

21

Who gives eve's replenishing board?
Who knows, who sees?
But the beating heart of Arthur's realm
dwells kindly over Camelot's king:
a royal priestliness chastely calm
knights the focus of our quests.

22

Oh, knightly self in heartbreak's
broken night,
of iron-plated breast and metal glove
and a visor which holds
the shadow from my face:
I to the day am knight,
to the night I am
a maid singing unheard songs.
Forlorn and bereft upon a turret height
I cannot lift my visor
nor cast away this spear towering
in my stony self.
Only a maid to day can knight
my maiden night
and with compassion's tear,
by kindliness neither bought nor begged,
call to this self spellbound
upon a tower of spells – and with
her word, breathing to embrace,
release this lost I's flow –
for my stony pinnacle of sleep
is severed from my day.

23

Oh, nightly self in heartbreak's
broken knight –
don't fall, don't waste your spear's quest,
wait quietly my love
my tears dissolve stone and metal bars,
reach out gaunt knight to me
I am a maid of day to maiden knight,
don't pine bereft and forlorn
upon that tower of cold,
don't douse yourself in doom
nor quail forgetful of our quest.
Quickly the pathway is unblocked
the stairs wind slowly down,
don't wait the way is winding
but is straight and true
beside me is the unlocked door
its guards sob with my sorrows,
fly my knight to me
and I will marry you to
day, come my night
the gate is open and the quest
is found – or will be found
when you and I
say, "We".

24
What did she whisper
flying from my second sight as dawn's
misty Celtic twilight dissolved
and colours hardened into things,
what did she say parting from me
this cold morning grey:
"When you and I
learn that togetherness lives
today".

* * *

In Autumn winds sways
a rosebud
with a blood-red crown

* * *

Cupid's Anon

This is sequence of linked poems which look toward the moment of falling in love – hence the title: Cupid's Anon

1

In breezes from far-off climes
dreams loosen one over one
unrecoverable as Autumn leaves

2

From childhood memories
into this moment
a butterfly flutters
to the blue flower.

3

By a glade behind whispers
alone and longing for a chalice
the greenery hides,
my finger bruises a slender stem –
and my heart is hurt
with another's hurt.

4

Dreaming till my eye
slips outward
seeing to be seen,
a face first shyly encountered
in a touch of eyes,
a face first loved
in that moment's echo
in the now.

5

A quiver from nowhere
an absence rhyming
with a presence –
a flight of muted recognition
with dart
of the I of an eye
in me.

6

The feathery focus
of not here
magnifies here.

7

A sensitive chaos:
Tremors
from a soundless bow
string reverberations
through a system's faltering
periodicity ...
in blithe and tender tempest
a child touches
the womb.

8

Drab turnings
round and round ambition's
merciless barren turn –
with ceaseless iterations
the Herod-in-me mutilates
time's new-born now.

9

Palaces of the wealthy are closed
to what is not
as it was.

In an unnoticed stall
the babe is born this night,
in caves woven with webs of human history
the infant smiles – and into
these stony double-spiralled stairways
sunlight shines
interceding for the in-between,
crowning with presence
what is yet to be.

10
And those other babes
those once fresh daytimes
in displaced days
wilted with the bitter myrrh
of innocence passed on,
tides unbecoming as incense
senses convolved in sense ...
as the golden glow of an eve gone by
is shrouded with interlude.

11
Yesterday's surface tinsel
pitched
with my turning sight
into memory's vat
of vagueness.

12
As drudgery habituates
and shrinks
the coming dream
as the vague displaces
vagaries ...

13
Then to then again
passed
before the future came
... to linger
as the happiness of time.

14
Until drawing through another
of many todays
Cupid's arrow flies.

15
Anonymous wings
bow minstrel music from
was to will be
through the love-riven heart
of the unfolding in-between.

16
Whispers from the winds
winged faces hover
as our first smile
blushes
with remembrance.

17
A first sigh pregnant
with the unforgettable promise
of someone forgot.

18
Our meeting focused by two moments
in a pause untimed –
sorrows in joy
two tears vault
arching through vanished time
toward
the happiness of now

19

The mystic troubadour:
through my swooning self
the beloved sighs –
the song in me is yours –
and yet I cradle still
within my tenderest time
the unknown you
I love.

* * *

From a white rose petal
a tear rolls
to coalesce with dew
upon the red rosebud

* * *

Colours in Chiaroscuro

Originally these poems were conceived as embroidering a single picture.

Whether they work as a poetic whole or whether they feel more like a haphazard collection of individual poems, I leave the reader to decide.

A recurrent theme is taken from Goethe's Theory of Colour: that colour comes into being in the dramatic interplay of light and dark – and by analogy black and white.

Avalon

When songs to imaginations are made
then here in Avalon a way is laid
dreaming through starry sometime climes
where maid and man without their shoes
seek sacrament in sweet débuts:
there behind those sleepy bedtime chimes
when now to a happily-ever-after cue
our prince and princess sigh to woo.

Topology

The mathematician cries:
When I was waking up this morn
as night from day was being torn
my thoughts curving such topsy-turvy waves
as stars descending into caves –
but then as though abandoned in my stall
a light within me wondered if the Fall
was but God's way
to give topology its say.

The Haekkelite replies:
I know exactly what you mean
from recapitulations in the human bean
when what's first made
is tenderly out-splayed
kneaded inside so nice and thin
as what's outside is turned within.

Knightly

Where is the narrow virgin way
between staunch kingly I
and queenly dress of you,
between this mantled
queenly quiet self
and you's brave kingly build?

Is the virgin way through night
the straight and narrow vertical
which crosses
(untrespassingly)
these horizontal lies.

The Blade in Stone

Burghers in a forgotten town
flexing huge grimaces of girth
lumber in file, gruntled with mirth
to flourish flabby fingers flush
around the crystal hilt clutched
by grey and gravid stone.

A sword lures their tortuous bustle
with contagious greed to grip its power:
a granite sheath (lust boils to pus)
"Just one gruff lurch of will
and I'll rip from rock's foster
the blade in stone –
and weigh all ways as mine
smelling this hour my ego
fills out all space and history,
this, this unbounded boundless me."

Each bows to rob
only to retreat,
blank life blinks
shuttering inflation
in a momentary niche.
Each sore with his sore
as palms lacerated by a diamond hilt
drip earthwards a healing red,
as speculations tingle
in a bruised self,
as eyes shuffle to the ground
from a centre tautened in pain.

(Only a youth, unknown
to the organising baton
of object-battened day,
bears in his pulse
a breathing name
burning its rune
on the blade in stone.)

Eddies

Of ways meandering
within mazes of appetite
where turns of eyes
and sweets upon the lips
or dainty sighs
and party wines in sips,
where pleasured snaps
spice up our girdling plays
– or as dripping taps
rap out the passing of todays.

Collisions

Frustrations giggling
tipsily round wine-soaked twirls
as two selves colliding
tie their not-there stares
... and plummet
through uncadenced rut
folded in flues of sweat –
still the other unknown
as before.

Anticlimax

In this retiring climax of operations
tempestuous with riteless stunts
bearing on our tiring brunts
all muffled up in ruthless grunts
where man dies in his coming
and woman hardly deigns to come.

Caprice

As random tune tandems
my inattentiveness with trivia,
as wine-bar wine whisks up
plays of perkiness
and memories are *cocktailed*
with presentiment ...

Seduction

Along this once-winsome
twisting road with Georgian
town-houses where I paraded
youth's unsought ideals
in free-fading Sixties' flowers –
and urges mowed
erstwhile tomorrows
into yesterdays.

Whistling tunes
that decorated days
which saw my adolescence
wave airily to childhood
fleeing far away.

Still wandering
this same winding way
where percy played and played
while wonder wound
away form wonderland –
and urges tied
what were tomorrows
into a hazy maze
of yesterdays.

The Highgate door opens
to a yesterday yuppie's
people-filled and over-partied den
"A friend of Simon's."
"Well, come on in!"

Dim electric lurid glare,
smoky passages, alcoves
where decorations and decorated
female searchlights coax
libido up from loveless surfaces.

My awareness touched
by a passing tactile arm,
mask-scarred eyes brush
through the party's pumped-up cool,
her smirking yet mildly pain-charred glance
sticks in mine,
capriciously the champagne glass
rolls on her moist-tongue smile,
she looks away (to let me know).

As though once more
in yesterday's time I
come on ...
practised exchanges
manoeuvring
our verbal intercourse.

Even here among
the yesterday yuppie's hangers-on
a third person can become a second
(a she becomes a you).

Electrifying strobo-haze
throbbing bobbing bass
roughs up vestibules of cool,
rapid repeating jingles beat up
the Sixties' rhythm into warmed-up
ecstatic techno-thrills,
dancing's no longer just a way
to say hello as on the floor
close up affectations
of pelvic sensitivity
are affected by the bonking beat.

Hard gets high on soft
and time is pressed ... till
in some dark smoky corner or on
a sportscar's springy backseat sponge
we begin to chug.

Tongues slurp in open lips
as we wildly exercising
drifts of our hands over us
approach the verge
where depths unexorcised
gape
around erection ...
as I unsteady in myself
lean on unsteadiness in you.

Did the Sixties' too soon aged youth
first conceive philosophy in the
lonely loveless aftermath
of a shag?

Late Sixties' rampaging fun hanging
over a millennium's ending
and new beginning –
tell me, in the last century's
last third what was not flowering
(and deflowered) in the Sixties?

Am I living in a new millennium?

Did it happen, did we
meet and chug last night
or was it some spent-youth recollection,
or did I just dream about a girl
I never had the courage to address
an imagined encounter, an emblem
of studied masturbation –
or was it allegory
the Sixties' flower of youth
seduced, shagged out
and pensioned off, idealism
smouldering to ashes ...
or was it presentiment
of wastage yet to come
in this world shackled by the sterile
Second Law of warmth's
(and human warmth's)
final entropy?

Who now from the Sixties
would dare a journey through the dark
to find that spring where
wells the Silver Stream
and follow its course toward
the Lady in the Golden Wood?

Captivity

Mirrorings of digital imprisonment
where we (you and I)
daub ourselves
in electric sight-sound fluctuations
soft-screech images on the
screen or virtual 3D
... days cloned
on wake-up pills
vitamin-bomb pills
'happy pills', zap-game 'pills'
damp-down pills –
with viagraesque virtuosity
rapping on p-pill-stifled wombs
before sleeping pills
bring slumber's zombie snores
... while the global web is wove
and from the dollar's pyramid
the sleepless Eye of Baradûr
stares ...

Entropy

Is this but echo
forgotten ere forgot,
blank pictures where an eye
casts no I,
where a self
habituated to the habitat
of surfaces reflectable
in a looking glass,
where an I shorn of
you asleep in me
(me sleeping in you)
is signed and numbered
as a normal personality –
that consciousness lashing its stick
of sex and sterile anonymity
through a world glowering with ego.

Heavy with hung-over sense
gravity downs hours
and meaning discontinues
in amalgams of separation
as vocal sounds called mine
murmur over
my ever extending incognito
as an I
caked in me
(cracking to be free)
cloys
exteriors of second persons,
as my hereditary conditioning
(the Herod-in-me)
lurks at the brink of sleep
and with automated response
takes pain- and daytime-killing pills
to slay that still small voice
which suffers and travails
for the child lost in my limbs.

Mechanic pound
of heartless brazen pace,
have I drummed out
childhood's accordance
in heavy phraseless beat
and with heavy even tramping
stamped out thankless iterations
of this selfsame ego ...
from a day of coolness
to a night of cold.

Mechanic sounds spinning
repetitions inside repetitions,
mechanic mounds of ongoing
endless monotony ...
have I rolled out my years
as sequential snakes?
Where, aged by worn out drives,
meaning commutes
toward probability
and laws of chance demand
grey entropy
or that slow decline
toward
the closet of
'sans everything'.

Treadmills

In electric-lit hours
memory miming masquerades –
have I mangled
now's news
to turns of yesterday?

Treadmills devoid of
respite-touches tapering
from unborn night
to flame in time ...

The While

Have I wiled away
the mystic while?

The mystic present:
where in our each heart's encounter
my life touches you
as your life touches mine.

Rainbows

In me your picture's secret
paints as unseen form,
never still yet ever
still beyond my sight –
my vision opening to light
chances or is chanced
to meet with prayer,
when preying fades away,
which looks from somewhere
out to somewhere
these looks of mine which
meeting another's glance
tremble to return;
my heartbeat patiently impatient
when sad in joy
or troubled through delight.

Within my painter's sight
rainbows
come to earth and linger
as promises from paradise –
the spectrum's seven
christen
the separated nearness
of black and white.

The brushstroke listlessly laments
as black descends on white –
am I Othello
who painted pictures of human war
for pity welling in her inner sight
when she seeing wounds
imagined me
and I seeing tears
saw her I?

Black on white:
White – virgin or barren?
Not yet virgin and surely
the barrenness is mine alone –
in this life where charcoal
memories engrave
chiaroscuro moods.

Are you out there
or in me?
Or am I moving
married to both?
To cries of inwardness that yearn to live
though sick with passion's dregs
smothered by cool-warmth –
or wed to outward wonders
woven as a world
where I, seemingly, am
yet am not.

Once I sketched these lines
as whispers from that voice
tacitly pining
as my colours drizzle
through chiaroscuro:
Borne in my I
before my birth
your picture looks
through countless outer forms
... until
meeting with a future now
the unseen beloved sees
to see in me –
the eyes in me are yours –
Maya's dark arthritic claws
are lost in fires uncindering ...
two flames flame
as one
and separate
as I to I
... beatific moments
passing slowly into time

Beatific togetherness
transcending
the monotone transience of time.

Yet my present-now is lame
and lives by this faith alone:
the future to the past is hope
but the future of the present charity.

Aged I plod the earth and paint
with eye and inner eye
but today as thence your face
dances in my shades
still fresh as roses
glowing luminously red
on Winter's bare
and blackened bark.

* * *

Through many guises, many lives
I have sought
the blue, blue flower
yet never knew
she had taken root
in the soft-scented earth
around my home
to watch so faithfully
my star.

* * *

... may a star shine upon our parting